FATSO

WRITTEN BY

BRANDIE GRASSO

INTRODUCTION:

A riveting story based upon real life struggles with weight loss. For anyone who has ever felt fat. This book will inspire you to lose weight.

FATSO

Introduced to this world in 1975 at St. Mary's Hospital in Southeast Texas, I was the third child in a prominent Sicilian family. My great grandfather came over from Sicily sometime in the 1900's. He was a fisherman and wound up starting the seafood packing industry on the Gulf Coast. Later on in life, my father inherited the business. The shrimp business somehow turned into a big oil company. Our last name was on the side of 18 wheelers and those big refinery tanks. I was too young to know all the logistics of Dad's business, but I did know it was big, really big. We lived in a beautiful house on the corner of course. All of us were beautiful, too. "The Movie Star Family", that is how some referred to us. My parents at that time were social. My mom was in the junior league, and ran the orphanage. We were strict Catholics who attended church every time the doors opened. All of us went to Catholic School. We looked like the model family. People wanted to be like us. Little did they know, we all were miserable behind the doors of that beautiful house!

There are four children. The oldest is 9 years older than I am and the most beautiful. Her body and face are flawless. A drag queen once came up to me at a gay bar and said "are you Lisas little sister?" I said "yes", and he said "OMG I wanted to be her"! Jon, who is 8 years older, is ridiculously good looking, and my idol. He has a great body and a chiseled face. Then me. I couldn't care less what I looked like, even early on. I have dark brown hair that was long and constantly in a pony- tail, and thick bi-focal glasses. All I wanted to wear were t-shirts, blue jeans, haas hat and cowboy boots. They called me a tomboy. I liked it when they called me that. Some say I am the most beautiful one, but I beg to differ. Last but not least, Lauren. She was the "baby" of the family, beautiful just like the others, and skinny!

School is a great way for me to chronicle my life. That's because I hated it so much. I started kindergarten at an Episcopal School, where my older sister and brother were attending. I cried so much that the kindergarten teacher sent me downstairs to the preschool and actually put me in a baby crib. The only thing that calmed me down was juice and graham crackers. When my mom caught wind of this, she removed me from the school. So I switched from Episcopal school to St. Patrick's Catholic School. I had an extremely difficult time letting go of my mom when it was time for school. The separation anxiety was horrible! I can remember clearly how it would all go down. I'd wake up, get dressed, and head down stairs for my mom to pull my hair up in a pony-tail. As we all headed towards the car after breakfast my stomach would start to hurt. The car ride would start off okay. I would always pray she'd drop me last. As we approached the first school, my heart would start to race. One more drop off and then me. When she pulled up to my school the tears would start automatically. She tells stories about having to peel me off of her, just to get me out of the car. Sometimes they would just push me out! It got too hard for my mom to drop me off, so my dad started taking us. He was very sweet with me, walking hand in hand all the way to the steps. I would tear up, but nothing like with my mom. Once inside, and with my friend Todd the anxiety would stop. My mom would always call the school principal in the morning to check and make sure I was ok. Sure enough, each morning someone from the office would peer in the classroom window.

Kindergarten at St. Patrick's grew less scary as time went on. I became comfortable with my teacher, friends and loved all the field trips we took. It was the most fun. I remember having in school. We had a nap time, snack time and we got to color. I thought this was not a bad way to spend my day. Things were good for me in kindergarten. Life was good at home from what I remember. I was having a fun childhood. At the time it seemed normal.

At school and home my friends were always boys. Our neighborhood was full of little boys. Three of my best friends lived on my street. I hated girlie stuff. The first time I invited a girl over to play, we got in a fight and she had to go home. Dolls and pink, yuck! The dolls were good for some things, like dismembering them. BMX bikes, cap guns and cowboy boots were my thing. I wanted to be a boy, or thought I was one. When my mom was not home and the Nanny was watching us, I'd sneak out of the house and ride around the neighborhood with my shirt off. I was totally obsessed with all of my dad's and brother's stuff! You name it - if they had it, I wanted it. Even down to their underwear. At that time I thought my dad and brother were the coolest guys on the planet.

In first grade there was a shift in the alignment at home. The coolest guys on the planet were not getting along. Jon had become a rebellious teenager. Not a good mix when your father is a total control freak. When they started fighting at home. I started to become withdrawn at school. I found it too difficult to concentrate on anything, so I daydreamed a lot. At times I even found myself praying. As Catholics, we were taught how to say prayers, but not how to feel the Holy Spirit or listen to God. For some reason when I prayed I would hear a whisper in my head. The first whisper I recall was while entering the school doors during second grade. I had just gotten out of my mom's car, and saw a girl who was bullied all the time drop her lunch box. As I got out of the car I watched a handful of other kids laugh as they ran right past her. He said "stop and help her", so I put my stuff down and helped her put everything back in her lunchbox. A warmness came about me, and it felt like everything was going to be okay. From that moment on the anxiety about going to school got better. I found early on that God would always make me feel better. That same school year, I was invited by the Catholic Church to have my feet washed by the Bishop. I knew it was special, but at that age it did not register how special. I remember thinking this is really cool, I get to wear my sandals without stockings to church! Then we get to go out to dinner all for me.

My father is a good man with a kind heart; however he ran our household like a dictator. He was not happy about anything. Constantly in a bad mood or easily put into one, especially if we made noise. He was always after my brother for something.

One morning all four of us were getting ready for school. I was about 7. For some reason I sneaked into my brother's room and stole a sticker off of his dresser. My brother got mad at me, so I started crying, then ripped the sticker in half. Without hesitation my dad came upstairs to see what all the fussing was about. He lit into my brother like I've never seen before. His eyes glowed like he was possessed, like the devil…….. They yelled and screamed, then started throwing fists at each other. My brother ran down the stairs and outside. We had to leave for school. Jon was sitting around the back side of the house crying. I was scared and crying!! My brother hated me, which made me even more scared. We all piled in my sister's brown Dodge Colt and off to school we went. I remember getting out of the car and walking in the school doors feeling lost, so lost! I don't think I said a word to anyone all morning, and daydreamed all day. This is also when I first remember living in total fear of my dad. Many years later I found out that the sticker was a one of a kind.

The fighting got so bad, that if Jon and my dad were in the same room it was like a time bomb waiting to go off, tick, tick, tick, BOOM! All of us waiting, just knowing they'd argue. I loved that my brother was able to stand up to my dad. He was my hero! Jon never made me feel fat. He did not try to change me like Lauren and my mom. I always felt safe around him. So I followed him everywhere. The fighting started to happen so often, it seemed there was no end. After Jon and my dad would fight, then my mom and dad would fight! With all the fighting going on, my parents came to the decision to kick Jon out of the house.

What a horrible Sunday evening that was. I sat upstairs on the balcony clinching my fists with my eyes closed, praying. Feeling overwhelmed with tears streaming down my face. Grandma came over right after Jon left the house. When she was told what happened, she cried. It was the first and last time I ever saw her cry. Seeing her so upset made me even more scared. I felt all alone; Jon was not home to protect us anymore. What could I do? Nothing. Too young to tell anyone; too young to fight back; so I devoured a bag of cheetos! The crunching silenced everything. The pain I felt went away for a minute. I prayed a lot extra that summer, for his safety, and that he would come home. Our family felt so incomplete without him. The quiet in the house, was not peaceful. It was filled with noisy tension.

The summer Jon was gone, I remember being over at my cousin's house. They invited me to go to a Whitney Houston concert. A few hours before the concert, we were changing in my cousin's room. I went to put on my jeans that fit the month before. The jeans would not zip. My cousin laughed at me, and said lie down. I did lie down. They zipped, but I could not breathe. She ran and told her mom. I felt like I was getting in trouble. My aunt called my mom, who had to go buy new jeans then bring them over. I was so embarrassed. All I remember about that concert was being too fat for my jean's, and the fact that my cousin told all of her friends that were coming with us what happened. I hid my tears behind the darkness of the concert. On the way home that night we stopped for a Hamburger. I think it was the first time I smiled the whole night.

Back then I often wanted to tell on my dad. I knew even at a young age that the way we were being treated was wrong. Who do you tell your feelings to when you eight years old? I told God! I was afraid no one else would believe me, because everything was portrayed to be so perfect in our house. So I would pray that he would just be nicer or that I could be smarter. As time went on I got smarter. I learned how to calculate my movement around his. At least he is a creature of habit. He would wake up and eat breakfast the same time every day. I knew to stay in bed until he drove off. Then he came home at 12 every day and would take a two hour lunch, always leaving the house at 2pm. From 2pm until 5pm whoever was home would surface, and if not home would come home. At 5:30pm, if I heard the rumble of his truck coming around the corner, I would run upstairs and stay in my room until the coast was clear. I would sit and listen to his footsteps. He would stop and take off his watch, and drop his change on the desk, then walk into the kitchen. He would graze for a minute and head into his office to go through the mail. Once he was in the office, I could sneak downstairs and out of the house without even having to say hello! I was simply avoiding an unpleasant encounter.

During the summer of fourth grade I started to attend camp. Not just any summer camp, but one of the best in the country. Camp was the greatest place on earth for me. I spent three weeks during the summer. Each day was packed full of activity. No dad to yell at me either. Some of my happiest times were spent at camp. Even with camp holding such a special place in my heart, it was still hard for me, for one reason, I was the fat kid! There were not many fat kids at camp, so I stuck out. In a cabin with 12 other girls, I was the only FAT girl. Being away from home, and doing so many fun activities was fabulous. It was so much fun I was able to power through the pain. I desperately wanted to just fit in, to hang out with the "cool" girls, but that did not happen often. The fat girl and the nerd of the cabin got to hang out together. On a daily basis someone would say something to me "why do you sweat so much", " you would be so pretty if you were skinny", "you should jump on the blob last so you can knock us all off", "I don't want you to bunk above me, you're too heavy" "fatso". Tough to swallow, especially without being able to run into the kitchen every time I got my feelings hurt or felt insecure. Let's just say I really looked forward to chow time.

At the end of each term, I was not happy about going home, but excited to see my mom and my dad for a few minutes. Even with the constant teasing, being at camp was better than being at home. I could feel the change in myself. My self-esteem would rise, because of all the things I was able to accomplish, like water skiing, rappelling, sailing, etc….. Due to being so active I would also lose weight, which was a big plus. Seeing my mom and dad arrive when it was time to leave camp was a mixed blessing. I was happy to see my mom. She would immediately recognize my weight loss and say something about it; unfortunately, it meant going home to what seemed like NO activity. It also meant living in fear of him again. It was inevitable that within an hour of the car ride home he would yell about something. I remember one year thinking I just want to get out of the car and walk back to camp.

For me food seemed to solve everything. If mom and dad were in the master bedroom fighting, I would head into the kitchen and quickly whip up a potato chip sandwich. The recipe was two slices of white bread, miracle whip, ruffles potato chips and a dash of cayenne pepper. After I quickly made the sandwich I'd make my way very quietly out the back door and into the garage. With the lights out in the garage, no one would see me. I loved the sound of the crunch. I would devour the sandwich, then head back inside like nothing happened. The recipe temporarily made everything all better. I did not know I had problem with food, until one afternoon I was over at my friend's house. His mom was inside baking cheese sticks from scratch to serve as finger food for her dinner party that evening. I can still smell the aroma, my mouth waters just thinking about those cheese sticks. When she finished baking she offered each of us one, before she headed to shower up for the party. The first one went down quick, too quickly I wanted another one., it was all I could concentrate on, I was determined to have another. So I told my friends I needed to go tinkle, and sneaked into the kitchen. Not just one, but I had two more! Mrs. Williams came outside after her shower and asked all of us who ate the cheese sticks, I hung my head and said I did!! I walked home that afternoon ashamed and scared. So scared that Mrs. Williams was going to tell my mom and worst of all my dad. All evening I sat with angst every time the phone rang, wondering if it were Mrs. Williams calling. She never did.

As problems continued at our house, my relationship with food got worse. At times it was all I could think about. When could I sneak my next snack, or have a meal? I constantly craved potato chips. Ruffles Sour Cream and Onion to be exact. They were the answer to all of my pain.

While I was in fifth grade my parents were having financial problems along with everyone else in the 80's. So it was my dad's idea to put us in public school. I was mortified the first day of fifth grade. Nobody was in uniform, no church next to the school, and I did not know a soul. We even had to change teachers throughout the day. That never happened in Catholic School. Math class was the worst. When called on to answer a question about fractions, all the kids laughed at me because I could not complete the equation. This was the first time math became a problem. One of the kids laughed at me and said "maybe four eyes can't see the board". Scared is how I felt. Totally out of place, like a fish out of water. No friends to turn too. During recess and gym class the other girls were so mean to me, calling me names. Fatso was a common one. I found myself not participating in any activities during gym and wondering alone during recess, or talking to someone who was not "popular". I remember sitting in class praying to God that it would all get better. It never really did get better for me in school. My relationship with food; however, blossomed into a full blown love affair.

Entering into the sixth grade, I was not the new kid anymore! At the time I even felt like I had a few friends. That all changed quickly. During picture day, one of my friends asked how she looked, and I said she looked like a third grader, not knowing that later on in the day my comment was going to float around the school, and that by the end of the school day none of my "new" popular friends were talking to me, not just for a few days, but for the remainder of the school year. If we had class together, they talked about me, made fun of my fat, called me fatso and four eyes, you name it…….. Since they picked on me about my weight, my mom decided it was time to see the pediatrician and put me on some kind of a diet. This was something I was supposed to be happy about? All I could do was cry on the inside. How could you take my food away from me, it was the only friend I had, it made me feel better when nothing else did. The word diet was a bad word. It meant that I was going to be even more different, when I already felt different enough.

I vividly remember the day of my first diet. Walking into the lunch room was scary. It meant I was going to get teased. I sat down opened my lunchbox pulled out my food, and immediately the other kids picked on me, ewww what is that, why do you have to eat that?   Are you on a diet, ha ha ha!! This went on for a while until I decided to eat lunch in the science lab. That's where the nerds would eat. The first week of the diet was miserable. I did not feel happy at all, and in fact, I felt totally depressed. Why couldn't I just be like everyone else, why couldn't I eat like all the other kids? I asked myself those questions relentlessly, so I started to do just that, eat like the other kids, I figured out that if I had money I could go through the lunch line and eat whatever I wanted. This would keep my mom satisfied and my food cravings satisfied. So most of the time I would have two lunches, the one my mom made me and the bag of chips and soda I would purchase in the lunch line. I don't recall losing an ounce of weight.

In eighth grade, we had to undress in the locker room in front of everyone. I loathed getting undressed in front of anyone. I hated my body. Changing in front of my mom was hard enough, but in front other kids it left me wide open for ridicule. Dressing out in the locker room was bad enough. Then I learned that the school housed an indoor swimming pool. In the spring time we would have to swim. How would I get myself out of this one? I got my mom involved. The pool looked and smelled like it was 100 years old. I knew that I had some leverage with my mom if I brought it to her attention that the pool was disgusting, and that her daughter was going to be swimming with every underprivileged kid in town. My real thoughts were there is no way I am getting in that pool. There is no way I am getting in a swimsuit in front of all my classmates. So I brought it to my mom's attention. She spoke with the principal of the school, and I started a job in the school library.

Some of the kids would have parties. I rarely attended these events with friends or a date. I would go by myself. When the close dancing would start, I knew that the popular good-looking boys would not ask me. I would wind up dancing with the ugliest boy in the group, or no one at all. I did not really care about the dancing part, I really did not care about boys either. Once we all hit puberty, our friendships shifted. The boys only wanted to be friends with the pretty popular girls in hopes of making it to first base. I started to become friends with some of the popular girls. The fact that we were rich helped a lot. Even though I was fat, I still had cute clothes. With very little interest in them, I would be known to give my clothes away. This giving of things quickly gained me popularity and some new friends.

Sometimes my mom would nag me about my weight loss. In eighth grade I am not sure what kind of diet I went on; however, I do remember losing weight because I was riding my bike a lot, just out of boredom. When my girl- friends were busy making out with their boyfriends, I would have nothing left to do, but ride my bike. My mom desperately wanted me to be thin before I went to high school. So she tried to motivate me with new clothes. The deal was for every 5lbs I lost, I got a new outfit. The first outfit I got was a pair of Esprit shorts with matching shirt. I wore the outfit to school, feeling proud of my accomplishment. While walking down the hallway to class two girls behind me said under their breath "the shorts would look better if she would lose five more pounds". That one comment sent me spiraling backwards. I even stopped riding my bike. Why should I try so hard? I still get picked on. Just a few little words and I let all of my hard work go down the drain. Gaining every pound back. My mom would say things like, "you don't want to start high school fat!" Even that hurt my feelings. When my feelings got hurt, I would just eat more.

Being fat meant I had something in common with my dad. In fact I tried to be as much like him as I could. This tactic seemed to keep me out of his aim. We both liked to eat! He would even take the fall for some of my night time grazing! Leftovers at our house were irresistible. I still salivate thinking of my mom's chicken fried steak. I knew that if we had leftovers he would be grazing too, so I would rarely get caught. In the morning my mom would see that the food was all gone, and immediately get on to my dad for eating so much. I would giggle on the inside. In a way, it was pay back for me to hear him get bitched at by my mom for his food intake, a secret I kept all to myself.

The worst was when my parents were dieting too. This usually meant no junk food in the house. Taking the snacks out of the house was like taking away my favorite toy. I would get so depressed. It was hard to binge with no snack food. Cooking food took too long to satisfy my immediate need. I found that eating a stick of butter dipped in brown sugar, was fast and satisfying, or anything dipped in mayonnaise. Ordering pizza and hiding it underneath my bed while no one was home also worked.

It turns out my mom was right. High school sucked. I have a few highlighted fun moments, but most of my memories are painful. My first freshman formal, the guy I asked to take me brought another girl along. He came to the door like a gentleman, but when I went to get into the front seat another girl was there. Of course I blamed myself!! I was not good enough. Every year there was going to be at least one formal I would have to attend in a dress with a date. For four years, it was agony every year around my sorority's formal. Yes, we had stupid sororities in high school. My sophomore year about two months before the formal, my mom asked if I wanted a new dress. I said no, I will just wear the one from last year. Having been under so much pressure to find a date, I started eating a lot. I ate so much that the week before the formal I tried on my dress, it was too tight! I thought YAY now I don't have to go to that stupid formal. For some reason the day of the formal, my mom made me try on the dress early that morning. She saw it did not fit and was furious with me. Why did you wait so long to tell me, she asked? I had no answer. I did not know how to tell her that it was too painful for me to go. I hated being the fat girl, in a big fat dress. So instead of being with the sorority girls setting up for the formal, I was out shopping for a dress with my mom. My weight fluctuated so much, that my mom did not want me to buy a dress, so we rented one. I loathed the dress we found, but pretended to like it so we could just get this debauchery over with. We got home with enough time for me to start getting ready. She went to the store to buy me panty hose, and ran into one of my sorority sisters. Of course she asked why I was not helping set up for the formal, and my mom told her it was because my dress did not fit, and I had to get a new one. When my mom told me she told Amy that, I almost cried. Great, now the whole sorority knew I was too fat for my dress!!! My date picked me up, I looked like a puffy Cinderella. Instead of heading directly to the formal, we decided to have some beers and do something fun, Chris happened to have a 22 rifle in his back seat, so we shot cans for a while before we went to the formal. That was the best part of the whole night. I walked into the formal and within ten minutes walked out. I ran into Amy during that ten minutes. She immediately said I saw your mom today, she told me why you were not here!! Her words sounded to me like she was saying, ha ha, I know your dress did not fit, because you are too fat!

On Friday nights my freshman and sophomore year, when my friends had dates with their boyfriends, and my parents would go out to dinner, I would stay home and eat. Jon and Lauren both went away to school. My little sister's social life was much better than mine, she was popular! So I was home alone a lot! The pantry became my friend. We had every snack food available, so I would start with a bag of chips, then on to crackers, and probably some sort of cookie. After the pantry, then the refrigerator to wash it down with a diet Dr. Pepper. For a while I would feel better inside. So I'd go and watch a movie, finding myself repeating the binge a few more times before I finally would feel guilty, and tell myself no more. A lot of lonely times back then.

My sophomore year I was walking to Geometry class. Some kids I knew were walking behind me, I heard them snickering about something. Apparently I had a new nickname. They were calling me camel hump ass.

Obviously my self-esteem was horrible. I did my best to try and pretend to be happy and put up a good front most of the time, but I was really and truly miserable. Miserable on the inside no matter where I went. If I bumped into someone in the hallway, I would feel too fat. I always, always felt too fat and not good enough! So miserable that I thought about ending my life often. My dad collected guns, most of which he kept in his closet. No one was home one afternoon, so I went into the master bathroom, opened dad's closet drawer and stuck a 9mm in my mouth, but could not pull the trigger. I couldn't do it to myself. I could not kill myself. That would be just stupid. It would hurt too many people. So I put the gun away quickly and never did that again.

In school I would stare off into space. It was so difficult for me to pay attention. My brain would just drift off into no man's land. Most of the time just dreaming about being skinny, and all the things I would accomplish once I was skinny. Thank goodness I was not stupid. I knew exactly what I had to retain in order to get by. My grades were not important to me at all. Nothing seemed to be important too me.

The summer before my junior year in high school, my brother moved back to Galveston. He and my father were trying to mend fences. Jon was being groomed to take over my dad's business. We spent time together like when I was younger. Things started to take on a sense of normal. My brother decided he wanted to help me lose weight, so he put me on a strict diet, and we started running a mile every evening together. He helped me tremendously, I lost 30lbs and felt good about myself, my mom was happy, everyone gave me lots of attention, I even gained a few friends along the way. The school year was looking bright. It was bright until one day about mid-way through my junior year, my best friend came over to my car and asked if I were ok. In fact everyone kept asking me. I said yes, I am fine. She asked if I had read the paper. I thought that was a funny question, since most high school kids did not read the newspaper. She said, take me home after school today and you can read our paper, it is something about your brother. Turns out he was arrested for selling drugs. That afternoon after finding out, I was upset that no one told me so I walked into our house mad. No lights were on, I found my mom in the master bedroom sobbing. I wound up comforting her. That's when she told me what happened to Jon I said I know, I read it in the paper!

Jon went on to serve two years in a federal prison camp. It was a weird time. I remember our whole house feeling like a dark empty cave Living in a small town did not help matters. People talk!! My mom lost friends, I lost friends, I also felt like I lost Jon. We spent our holidays traveling to El Paso to visit him. I went to visit twice, that was all I needed. It was just too hard. Way too hard seeing him in that place. Nobody in our house was happy. During that time I got fat! Really fat!

Adding to my unhappiness, I was changing schools again. Math is not my subject, and standardized tests are brutal. In order to graduate from high school you have to pass all portions of standardized testing. For four years I could not pass the math portion. I went to countless tutors. Attended workshops, nothing worked. Mentally I was blocked. It just did not compute! Generally after a tutoring session, I would go straight home and eat a bag of chips, anything to soothe my mental anguish. Potato chips, were always my immediate go to! Ruffles and Lays were my friends.

Not only was I starting my senior year at private school, I would also have to attend with my very popular little sister. She was the girl that everyone wanted to be. I even wanted to be like her. At least skinny like her. Life felt so unfair. Why did I get the fat gene? Being the new girl at school my senior year was dreadful. The girls and boys in my class had been in school with each other since kindergarten. They were nice to me, but I did not have the same bond with them that they had with each other. So I felt alone a lot.

One afternoon while by myself, I tried lying out on the seawall. So I put my lawn chair out facing the beach. I lay down quickly, I did not want anyone driving by looking at me. Let's just say I looked ok in a one piece if I were laying down. Just as soon as I got comfortable a car full of guys I went to school with drove by and yelled "beached whale" as they sped past me. I was super embarrassed, and thankful no one else was with me. So I continued to lie out. My philosophy is tan fat looks better than white fat!

As the years past my fathers binge drinking got worse. When he drank too much his temper would flare to it's worst. While in high school I remember a handful, of nights that my mom packed us up to stay the night in a hotel or at a friend's. He was a mean sloppy drunk. One night really stands out in my mind. He came home drunk from the office. That's how these events normally unfolded. This time he came home, and then went back out. He came home a second time. Things got ugly between him and my mom. They were screaming at each other in the kitchen. Lauren and I sat upstairs on the top step yelling at him to stop. The more we yelled the worse it got. He started throwing everything out of the refrigerator he could find at my mom. Then he went into the bathroom and hit his hand up against the wall. He broke his hand that night. My mom took him to the hospital, he came home and went back out again. We packed up that night, taking the dog too, in fear he would harm anything that got into his path. The morning after my mom dropped us off at school late. My friends asked where I had been all morning. I lied and said at the dentist! Lauren and I were both told to lie about how my dad broke his hand. Lauren and I staid the night over at my grammas house, when mom and dad picked us up, I knew she was going to ask about his hand. She did and he lied. That moment made me so angry, angry enough to eat two big bags of Ruffles.

High school finally ended. My weight topped off at 200lbs. I remember graduation day. I felt like a hot air balloon in my red cap and gown. I just wanted to get graduation over as quickly as possible. A new beginning was around the corner for me. I would be starting Jr. College It turned out to be worse than starting fifth grade. I did not know anyone. All of my friends went off to college. I was lost and scared all over again. There were some benefits. I had more freedom. Still living at home with the dictator was difficult at times, but I could go a week without seeing him. Being older meant I had my own money. This opened up a whole knew world of binge eating for me. One of my favorite times was Sunday morning, when I was really supposed to be in church, I would be praying to the golden arches. I would drive thru and order a kids meal with burger and fries. Then drive to the Seawall and eat it. You could order whatever you wanted without anyone seeing you do it. I thought the concept was brilliant. Drive up, order food, eat in the car, and the throw away the evidence. What a fantastic concept! There were times I ordered food to be delivered when no one was home. I would hide the evidence underneath my bed and sneak it out with me the next day to the trash. In college there was enough time in between classes to go out for lunch. My favorite spot was a local Italian restaurant. Sometimes I would eat there three times a week. I became so regular, that I had the same waitress every time and I did not even have to speak to her. She would just bring me what I wanted. A large glass of ice tea, basket of fresh garlic bread, and a bowl of angel hair pasta in garlic butter. For a whole hour out of my life, I felt important.

With no end in sight my weight kept climbing. My clothes started coming from Lane Bryant, the fat girl store, as my mom referred to it. Life was humiliating for me. Very casually one morning while riding in the car, mom asked would you ever think about joining a program like Jenny Craig. With tears welling up in my eyes, I swallowed hard then said yes.

At 19 Jenny Craig became what was just the tip of the ice berg for me and my dieting career. Anytime I tried something I would be slightly successful. I would get half way to my goal and then get comfortable with my weight, and stop dieting, and then within months gain it all back. All I wanted to do was eat like everyone else, not be such a spectacle all the time. If I went out to dinner on certain programs, I would have to bring my own food. Then be asked, "why are you eating that"? It was hard enough being fat, without having to explain to every Tom, Dick and Harry what I was eating it for. Honestly, wasn't it obvious why I was eating differently from everyone else? This happened to me for ten years. YoYoing all the time. You name the diet and I have tried it. All of them worked to a degree, but I never went all the way!! The most ridiculous one was when I was seeing a doctor who was actually prescribing me speed. I'd lose weight, get off the pills, then gain it back quickly.

My whole world started to revolve around weight loss. One time my parents negotiated with me. They said if I lost 20lbs on my own that I could get lipo-suction. I agreed and hit the gym. Soon it was off to see the plastic surgeon. I was so excited! That is until I got to the appointment and had to get naked in front of the doctor and the nurse. I had to stand in front of a video camera, so she could record my whole body. It was for me one of the most humiliating experiences EVER, I never got naked in front of anyone! I was so embarrassed for her to see me, all of me. She asked about the bump on the back of my butt, (my camel hump) which turned out to be a fatty tumor. She was asking if I wanted it removed. Without hesitation of course I said YES!! The surgery went off without a hitch. Within a few weeks people could really start to see a difference. Combined with my new contoured body, I started a high protein diet, and hit the pavement. In months I was able to wear a normal size. A size 10. That was small for me. For a little while it was even a size 8, but that did not last for very long.

After Jr. College, I attended a trade school and earned a degree in Computer Science. The fifteen month program I attended was tough. During that time, I worked for my dad, and lived at home. The stress level was almost unbearable at times. I am not sure which was harder school, or working for my dad. When I started the program, I was a size ten. By the end of fifteen months I was a size twelve. Once I graduated from the program, I got a job working in downtown Houston. What a relief, I was able to move out! I staid an average size for a long time. Life was easier living alone. I could finally breathe. No more walking on eggshells. Everything was good, I had a career, nice place to live, but still a bad body image. Often times I would be invited to parties or work functions and would not attend. I hated the way I looked. I would have a good week with food, then a bad one. The yo yo dieting was still happening. Every month I would try something new. Lose five pounds, feel good about myself, then go back to my old eating habits. What I needed was something totally different. New scenery, so I applied for a job in Austin.

After the first three months of living in Austin I got into good shape. I became very active. Instead of staying inside, I had new things to explore. Hiking the green belt became one of my favorite things to do. My apartment was close to my job, so I rode my bike back and forth to work. The grocery store was around the corner so I walked to buy groceries. It was a different way of life for me. My size 12 pants started to feel big. Life was feeling great. That is until one afternoon while sitting in a turn lane, I was rear ended. The car accident injured my back so badly that I could not exercise for months. My activity level dropped. I started to eat more and more, because there was nothing else to do. Within five months, I went from a size 12 to a size 16. Devastating for me! Depressing, why was this happening to me again? I worked so hard to change and get where I was. How could I go so far backwards? There was no end in sight. I finally gave up on myself.

I took on a new job after my back healed from the accident. It was a traveling position. I was gone a lot. This meant lots of eating out. For two years I traveled every week. I gave into my addiction and gave up the battle. Food started to rule my world. I could not stop eating. It became the only thing I liked to leave the house for. The binging went from once a week, to huge meals three times a day! I would wake up in the morning and have a huge breakfast out, 2 eggs, hash browns, bacon, biscuits and huge glass of ice tea, lunch beef enchiladas, rice, beans, basket of chips, queso, ice tea, snack a big bag of chex mix, dinner, appetizer, salad, steak potatoes and dessert, all of this for myself in one day. Enough food to feed a family of three for the day. I hated myself, the way I felt, the way I looked, but I could not stop eating.

I was living in complete denial. I thought somehow if I wore baggy clothes, it was okay. If my fat did not poke through the clothes, then no one could see that I was fat. A delusion I created for myself, so I could live with myself. The truth is I was fat. Fatter than I had ever been before. Consumed by fat!

 The desire to change became suffocating. A little whisper kept going off in my head, "you have to lose weight", you have to. So I started the climb again.   This time I could do it.   In the morning, I would wake up, with the attitude that it was a new day! During that new day, I knew I needed to exercise, and eat right. I needed a good solid routine. I'd stay on a routine for about 4 days, then be called out of town for business.   All of the bad for me food in the world at my finger tips, with an excuse to eat all of it! I'd still say to myself you can do this. You can wake up in the morning and work out at the hotel, and eat sensibly. Day one would always go well. Then after working long hours, it would be impossible to motivate myself to do as well on day two. Eventually I would say to hell with it and sabotage myself by having a large meal.

My wake up call happened on the road. While on business in Kansas, US Airways lost my luggage. So I had to buy new clothes. What is it about new clothes, they just don't fit like my old ones. That day I bought a pair of mens jeans that were a size 40. This was the first big reality check. The second was when I noticed the seat on the airplane started to feel snug and I had to lengthen the seat belt. The third was while walking through the airport I noticed that an elderly woman was walking much faster than I was. I tried to keep up with her, but could not. What was wrong with me? How did I get to this awful place?

My health started to deteriorate. I was sick all the time, and when I was not sick I still did not feel good. Things started happening to my body, my hands started to tingle. I was not sleeping very well. I had no motivation! Something within my body was going wrong. I went to the Dr. and found out that I weighed 223lbs, was borderline diabetic and had high blood pressure all at age 29. After I learned the direction my health was headed I got scared. Desperately I wanted to change, but was not sure where to even start. The doctor put me on an antidepressant, hoping that elevating my mood would stimulate weight loss. All that stuff made me want to do was kill myself.

So I got off the pills and started to pray. I prayed for where to seek help. This time the whisper said turn to your father for help. Not the holy father, I had already done that, but my dad. Of course I listened. I composed an e-mail, telling him the story about the old lady passing me up in the airport and how insecure I felt. He replied compassionately, suggesting that I try something more aggressive, like stomach surgery. Wow, I never thought he would be open to actually doing something for me, considering he had already spent a small fortune trying to help me. I weighed out my options. It seemed like I had two choices, a personal trainer or Bariatric Lap Band Surgery. My mom felt like I should go with the personal trainer. She felt like I could do it without surgery. My dad felt like I needed something more aggressive. I felt like my dad was right. I knew in my heart that he could relate to my battle. So I attended a seminar that explained all about the surgery. Then made an appointment to meet with my surgeon. After that I got lined up for a battery of different tests. Once the tests were completed, the surgery was scheduled. My whole life was about to make a permanent change.

This time I wanted to succeed for myself. Nothing was going to get in my way of reaching this goal. No relationship, work, nothing! My complete and total focus was on achieving my ultimate dream. I was going to lose 100lbs, and finally be happy!

It was like being a newborn. I had to learn how to eat all over again. First two weeks of soft food. My stomach was still healing on the inside so I could not eat solids. The two weeks came and went and I was already 11 lbs down. It was now time for solid food. I could not wait to chew something other than ice. My first solid meal was at a restaurant, I ordered exactly how my nutritionist said. Chewed my food 30 times and did not drink with my meal. That seemed to be the trickiest part. Simply because no one understood the concept, so then I would have to explain. About a month into things I was able to exercise. There is a big mis-conception, that when you have stomach surgery you just lose weight without any effort. That's not true. Not true if you want to achieve your total goal.

With over 25 years of experience in losing and gaining weight, I actually gained some knowledge. I knew I could not just hit the trail running. If this was going to last I would need to start things at a turtle's pace. With my past attempts at weight loss, one of my biggest problems was combining eating healthy with exercise. I would generally do one or the other. As a fat person exercise scared me. It scared me because I felt like I was setting myself up for failure. I always felt insecure inside a gym. All of those fit people working out smiling. It seemed like all eyes were on me as I walked in the door. I was not fit or smiling. For me going to any public place to exercise was not a good idea. I did not want people to see my fat jiggle. I would not push myself as hard with everyone watching. Onlookers should be more motivating, but I was too insecure with my body to have anyone looking at me.

The workouts started with simply walking my dog casually around the neighborhood. Early on I knew that I would have to have something to hold me accountable for exercising. So for my birthday, I asked for a puppy. His name is Willie. He woke me up and got me moving even when I did not want to. Interestingly enough, Willie has a problem with food. He is an over eater just like his mom! I made a promise to myself that I would wake up every morning and walk him. Then at lunch time I would take a casual walk around the building. A few months went by the walking turned into a light jog, just in the neighborhood. So now I was walking the dog and going for a short jog. Before I knew it, my energy level started to increase. I wanted to be outside more. In my head I would set little goals for myself, I can make it to this light pole today on my jog and stop. Eventually, I made it to the hike bike trail and could jog more than one mile without stopping. This was huge for me!! Now, I am jogging the trail, walking the dog, walking at work, and starting to ride my bike instead of drive.

My emotions were all over the map. Sometimes during a run I would burst into tears for no reason. The tears would flow and I would just run harder. The harder I ran the more I trampled all those years of pain.

The weight was starting to fall off. All of my clothes were too big most of the time. I would buy new ones, and within weeks need more. Not too much longer and I would reach my goal. I felt a plethora of emotions. Happy, sad, scared!

Small changes started to happen everywhere. At work I could not sit still. If I got bored I took a walk around the building. I noticed that I wanted to motivate others to do the same, I felt like I could help other people. It seemed like office butt ran rampant around my place of business. So I started to encourage my work mates to walk around the building with me. This lead me to the idea of starting a Health Club at the office. I wanted every fat person to feel what I was feeling, I wanted to give back the gift that was given to me. So I wrote a letter to the president of the company. He thought it over and said it was a great idea. So a small committee was formed and the Health Club was born. During the announcement of the Health Club to the entire company, the president stated that it was his idea. This really irritated me. I was so up and happy about the whole thing, and then I allowed him to steal my thunder! That evening when I got home, I did not feel like exercising. I felt like eating, eating a lot, gorging myself. There I was in the kitchen, attempting to eat anything I could get my hands on. I don't remember what I munched on, but do remember it not tasting good. This was the first time in my life that food did not taste good. No satisfaction in anything I ate, I tried biting into a lot of different things. It was the strangest feeling. I was able to take Willie for a walk instead of stuffing my feelings. Food did not soothe me anymore. My relationship was over.

More accomplishments were to come. While out on a bike ride one evening, I decided to stop over at a friend's house. At this point I was 20lbs away from my goal, and super determined to get there. When I walked in the door her sister was over. She mentioned a 10k race coming up and said I should do it with her. After some convincing I said yes. So I started jogging every day with only a month to prepare. Each day it seemed like the running was getting harder. Finally I broke mile three and things got a little easier. Sometimes I would think, I have to run three more, I don't really want to, but then I would tell myself "I think I can, I think I can"…… Eventually I ran six miles without stopping. For me that was just huge! The people on the hike bike trail must have thought I was nuts. For the whole month that I trained for the 10k, every time I ran, I would cry. Shedding years and years worth of pain, sometimes the tears were tears of joy, in aw of what I was accomplishing! Race day came quickly. I woke up emotional, so proud of myself for what I was about to do. I got there late, so I had to jump out of my car and just start running. The energy was like magic. The day before I saw my acupuncturist and asked her to make my legs feel light like feathers and for the rest of me to be strong like a mountain. I jogged proud, with my head held high, like I was running the Boston marathon. I knew it was only 6 miles, but it was the hardest 6 miles of my life. Finally I caught up with my friend. I was enamored by the energy and so thankful to my friend for the encouragement!! I stopped and walked with her for a minute, using the time wisely to drink water and cool off. I poured water into my baseball cap and threw it on my head, not realizing the guy behind us had a very expensive camera in his hands. I drenched his camera, was extremely embarrassed, so I saw that as my opportunity to start jogging again. The finish line was getting closer, sweat was pouring off of me, so I did it, with a huge smile, I took my shirt off, showed my scar and what tummy I had left to the world. I ran across the finish line without my t-shirt on, sports bra only, and burst into tears with a big smile on my face. Not only was that the first time I ran a road race. It was the first time in 30 years that I took my shirt off in public! The fact that I could take my shirt off, lit me up inside, boosted my self-esteem and motivated me so much that the last 20lbs seemed to melt off quickly. I remember the day I reached my goal. It was during the summer and I was at work on the scale that we purchased for the health club. It said 133lbs. I did not share the big news with anyone, I just looked up in the sky folded my hands and said thank you! My prayers were truly answered. Look at the gifts that had just been given to me, through my father nonetheless. God truly works in mysterious way's.

At that time my insides felt like a jet engine revved up. I had energy! Tons of it. My body's chemistry completely changed. I could not sit still. Concentrating on any one thing got harder and harder, because I wanted to do it all. There were times that I passed by the mirror and did not recognize myself. Old friends really did not recognize me. I even had family members that I had to say it's me silly! Transformed on the outside.

People started to treat me differently. My friends seemed mixed about the new me. Some were totally happy for me. Others almost acted jealous. Jealous of me, what the heck. I thought there was absolutely no reason to be jealous of me. That's just crazy. When I went out to bars, I got attention, that I thought I always wanted, but now that I was getting it, I had no idea what to do with it. I was uncomfortable in my new body. Why wasn't I on cloud nine? This was a dream come true. I was happy with myself, but I think almost in shock with what I had accomplished. I would cry myself to sleep most nights when fat, and just dream about being skinny. It was one of those dreams that I thought was for other people. Now here I am skinny. I knew I had been blessed, but just could not wrap my arms around what had just happened for me. Flabbergasted, almost in disbelief that this was really me and really my new body!!

Some people were snarky about my weight loss. They would say things like you took the easy way out. It is not the easy way out ever if you have to have surgery for anything. It is a brave thing to do. A last resort. I knew there was no end in sight for me, and

I needed something to control me. The surgery feels like getting hit in the stomach with a baseball bat. For a solid year my stomach hurt every time I ate something. I still had to watch what I ate, and exercise. Having the band is a safety net, it keeps you from binging; however if you are smart you can manipulate the band, stretch your stomach so you can eat whatever you want. I was lucky that things fell into place for me. I lost 100lbs without ever having to get the band filled to actually squeeze my stomach. This does not happen for most people, in fact it is rare.

A part of me was scared at what I had accomplished. I was scared to fail. In all the years past, I had gained the weight back plus some. What was different about this time? This time was different, because I wanted to do it for myself. My health issues were the driving force, but this time I wanted to lose the weight solely for me. Not for my mom, not for anyone, but me.

My whole life was changing. I felt like I was losing control. I started to question why, I was fat to begin with. These emotions lead me to seek therapy. I was eager to find out the "why's" about myself. As I did, the first 30 years of my life, became very clear. Instead of turning to drugs and alcohol, I abused food. I stuffed all of my emotions from the time I was 6 until I was 30. Once therapy was over with, I decided to embrace my new body and have fun with it. I bought a lot of new clothes. It was so much fun walking into a store and trying on a size 6. Once in a while it would register to me that holy shit, I was a size 20, now I am a size 6, then I would generally cry because I was filled with joy. I think about it in terms of people, I lost a whole person. It is a bizarre way to think of weight loss, but so true. The first time I wore a bikini was the craziest thing. I felt shy and a little bit self conscious, but got used to it quickly.

Life started to feel balanced, but with a new direction. I knew I wanted to help other people lose weight. I told myself that for a whole year after surgery, I would say a prayer for every obese person I saw. If in the grocery store or walking down the street, I found myself praying a lot. This lead to the desire to help more in a bigger way. So I offered some help to a friend who seemed like she was ready to shed her unwanted pounds. I very gingerly asked if she wanted my help, and shared a little bit of my story. I said, if you want to, start coming to my house once a week, and

I will help you lose the weight. She started coming over. The first week, we sat down and reviewed her weaknesses with food. Then I made a list of rules for the first two weeks of her new journey! I made it very clear to her that she was not on a diet.

My weight loss philosophy is to start slow. The whole turtle's pace thing that I did with myself. As a child while dieting I spent most of the time depressed. Taking everything I loved away from me all at one time was not the way to motivate me. Even as I started to lose weight, I still would reward myself with food I loved. Each week I expanded on those rules. The plan I put into action worked. She started to lose within the first week. As the weekly meetings continued, she looked better and better. Giving back what I learned for myself was working. I was tickled pink. As she started to lose her girlfriend started to lose as well. I helped them a long the way for a while, then they both lost the rest on their own. It was a magnificent thing to see. Both of them look and feel sensational. At that point I wanted to help as many people as I could. I tried to branch out, but it just was not happening. Then it came to me, that I needed to tell my story.

Today, I stand 5'4 139 pounds. I have been able to keep the weight off now, for five years. It feels amazing to be thin and even more amazing to be happy. I have even developed a plan that can help others accomplish there goals.

Listening to your inner voice is so important. Whether you get whispers from God, or whatever your higher power is. Listen to it. Don't give up on it. That voice will guide you. It will guide you on how to make your dreams come true.

Finding out why you have a food addiction is the number one way to heal it. If I never put it all together, that my childhood pain is why I stuffed so much down my throat I would be a fatso all over again. I now believe that the pain I felt as a child provided a foundation that has paved my eternal destiny. Without the pain I suffered. There would be no color in my life. No matter what the experience whether good or bad, they are all just blessings in the end.

If you have a friend or family member who is overweight, share this story with them. Let he or she know that they are not the only ones out there suffering from food addiction. If you have questions or need help, please visit www.fatcoach.net. The weight loss battle has inspired me to become a consultant.

THE END

Made in the USA
Columbia, SC
11 June 2019